ideals®
MOTHER'S DAY
2006

Dedicated to a celebration of the American ideals of faith in God, loyalty to country, and love of family.

Features

Departments

Cover: One of the rewards of a garden is the beauty of freshly cut flowers, gracefully arranged in a basket. Photograph by Dianne Dietrich Leis/Dietrich Leis Stock Photography.

Inside front cover: These delicate flowers are framed by the window in this contemporary painting entitled FLOWERS BY THE WINDOW LEDGE *by Boris Nicolaiev. Image from Fine Art Photographic Library, Ltd., London/Bourne Gallery Reigate/Gallery Gerard, Wassenaar, Holland.*

IDEALS—Vol. 63, No. 2, March 2006 IDEALS (ISSN 0019-137X, USPS 256-240) is published six times a year: January, March, May, July, September, and November by Ideals Publications, 39 Seminary Hill Road, Carmel, NY 10512. Copyright © 2006 by Ideals Publications. All rights reserved. The cover and entire contents of IDEALS are fully protected by copyright and must not be reproduced in any manner whatsoever. Title IDEALS registered U.S. Patent Office. Printed and bound in the USA. Printed on Weyerhaeuser Husky. The paper used in this publication meets the minimum requirements of American National Standard for Information Sciences—Permanence of Paper for Printed Library Materials, ANSI Z39.48-1984. Periodicals postage paid at Carmel, New York, and additional mailing offices. Canadian mailed under Publications Mail Agreement Number 40010140. POSTMASTER: Send address changes to IDEALS, 39 Seminary Hill Road, Carmel, NY 10512. CANADA POST: Send address changes to Guideposts, PO Box 1051, Fort Erie ON L2A 6C7. For subscription or customer service questions, contact Ideals Publications, 39 Seminary Hill Road, Carmel, NY 10512. Fax 845-228-2115. Reader Preference Service: We occasionally make our mailing lists available to other companies whose products or services might interest you. If you prefer not to be included, please write to IDEALS Customer Service.

ISBN 0-8249-1307-8 GST 893989236

Visit our website at
www.idealspublications.com

Give a Red Rose to Mother

Loise Pinkerton Fritz

Give a red rose to your mother—
A rose on this Mother's Day—
She who has loved you and raised you;
She who has taught you to pray;
She who through good and through lean times
Has constantly stayed by your side.
Give a red rose to your mother,
Oh, give a red rose to her, child.

Give a red rose to your mother,
Not only this day, but each day.
Sprinkle the velvety petals
With kind words of love and of praise.
For God gave us mothers so precious,
Though they be near or afar.
Oh, give a red rose to your mother,
The rose of a grateful heart.

The deep red of roses is highlighted by the simplicity of the glass table setting in this bright morning room. Photograph by Jessie Walker.

Treasures

Edith Tatum

While life is at the springtime,
I shall garner many things—
The song that in the morning
A joyous redbird sings;
The perfume of the lilacs
That the sighing south wind brings;
The softly silken shimmer
Of a field of young green corn;
The web a spider stretches
All dew-wet upon the thorn;
Long, slanting, lacy shadows
And the grass which they adorn.

Little House

Betty J. Silconas

Little house beside the road
Where children laughed and cried,
What gaiety and merriment
Your old walls held inside;
The seasons came,
The years all passed,
Those little children grew up fast
With love, beside the road,
Where seeds of joy were sowed.

Home, the spot of earth supremely blest,
A dearer, sweeter spot than all the rest.
—Robert Montgomery

The Elizabeth Perkins House in York, Maine, is a fine example of the
Colonial Revival style, popular in the early twentieth century.
Photograph by William H. Johnson.

Going Home

Craig E. Sathoff

It's always special, going home,
For there we're sure to find
A well-loved smile, a welcome hand,
A manner sweet and kind.
And going home is beautiful,
For though we've traveled on,
We still have ties innumerable
That link us with our home.
For those of us who can't be home
With any frequency,
We still have bonds to take us there
Within our memory.

We think of Mother's homemade pies,
A fort up in the tree,
Of baseball games and picnicking,
Of family unity,
Of little brother's steadfast love,
Of boyhood pets we knew,
Of fishing trips and gardening—
The thoughts are never few.
The thoughts go on and on—
I'm glad they never end;
For it is always good to me,
This going home again.

The Coin

Sara Teasdale

Into my heart's treasury
I slipped a coin
That time cannot take
Nor a thief purloin;
Oh, better than the minting
Of a gold-crowned king
Is the safe-kept memory
Of a lovely thing.

Exquisite roses fill this painting entitled FLOWERS BY THE WINDOW, by Boris Nicolaiev. Image from Fine Art Photographic Library, Ltd., London/Bourne Gallery Reigate/Gallery Gerard, Wassenaar, Holland.

Mother and Home

John Jarvis Holden

Mother! Home!—that blest refrain
    Sounds through every hastening year:
All things go, but these remain.

Held in memory's jeweled chain,
    Names most precious, names thrice dear:
Mother! Home!—that blest refrain.

How it sings away my pain!
    How it stills my waking fear!
All things go, but these remain.

Griefs may grow and sorrows wane,
    E'er that melody I hear:
Mother! Home!—that blest refrain.

Tenderness in every strain,
    Thoughts to worship and revere:
All things go, but these remain.

Every night you smile again,
    Every day you bring me cheer:
Mother! Home!—that blest refrain:
    All things go, but these remain!

Climbing roses frame the entry to this English cottage-style garden.
Photograph by Gemma Giannini/Grant Heilman.

HOMETOWN AMERICA

Arlene Siebold

INAVALE, NEBRASKA

In Willa Cather's *My Antonia*, ten-year-old Jim Burden, newly arrived from the east, looks out upon the Nebraska prairie in wonder. "As I looked about me," Burden later recalls, "I felt that the grass was the country as the water is the sea."

The same vision of endless prairie grasses greeted the pioneer families who came to Nebraska in the late nineteenth century. Like Jim Burden, they saw the vast sea of grass, but they also saw something more. In the endless grasslands they saw their futures. With faith and sweat they broke the prairie sod, carved fields for their crops, and built homes for their families. As more families arrived, little prairie towns sprouted up and small clusters of buildings huddled close together, dotting the low, rolling landscape.

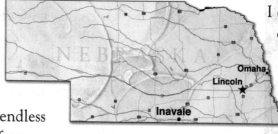

One such town was Inavale, in Webster County, where I lived as a child, near Willa Cather's childhood home. Located in southernmost Nebraska, in the Republican River valley, where once great herds of buffalo roamed, Inavale was the scene of my happiest childhood days.

We moved into Inavale from a nearby farm when I was nine years old. I had been near the end of my fourth-grade year at the Pleasant Prairie country schoolhouse, but there were no fourth-graders at Inavale's two-story, red-brick school. So the teachers made do with what they had and enrolled me in the end of fifth grade. The school, built in 1922, housed high school students upstairs and lower grades on the ground floor. I clearly remember being powerfully driven to prove that, even at nine, I could handle the hard work of fifth grade.

Everything in Inavale was within walking distance. In the business district were a grocery store, a barber shop, a bank, the post office, a small, two-story hotel, a lumber yard, a mercantile, a filling station, and the creamery. There were two churches in town, the Methodist church and, just a short walk away, the Christian church. Our home sat across the

---

On May Day, we would pick flowers to place in our May baskets.

---

street from the Methodist church. On Sundays we would walk over for services. We all met upstairs first; then the children would be dismissed to the basement. There, on small seats at low tables, we learned simple lessons from the Bible.

Everyone in Inavale looked forward to

Saturdays, when the town grew busy with local farm families who came to sell their milk, cream, and eggs and then buy supplies for the coming week. Some weeks there were free outdoor movies. Other Saturdays we gathered for square dances in an open hall above the mercantile. Fiddlers and guitar players provided the music. I was proud that my father was often one of the callers.

Spring and summer brought happy days to Inavale. On May Day, we would pick flowers to place in our May baskets, which we made from cardboard cartons and decorated with crepe paper or other showy items. What fun it was to sneak up to someone's door and leave a basket, then run and hide, breathlessly waiting for them to open the door and find the surprise.

On summer weekends, there were baseball games on a field just outside town. When an extra nickel was available, my parents would buy me a bottle of grape pop to drink while I watched the game. A nearby apple orchard provided plenty for all the children to eat.

In this small prairie town, our lives meshed together with those of our neighbors. The spirit of the hard-working pioneer families who had settled these prairies remained strong in the people of Inavale. We were a community who watched out for and cared for each other. My father was a carpenter by trade, but his job changed to suit the needs of our small town. He did all manner of repair work, whatever was needed. Once he even cut hair for those who could not afford the barber.

In the 1930s, the Great Depression brought difficult days to Inavale. Soon nature followed

Willa Cather's 1879 childhood home. Photograph by Jeff Greenberg/Unicorn.

with even more trials. The town survived, but many changes occurred that would never be undone. My family left Inavale for Lincoln when I was eleven years old.

I returned to Inavale for a visit as an adult. I took one of my sons and two of my grandchildren. I wanted to give them a sense of the land, of the wonderful freedom to be felt on the open prairie. I wanted them to understand where my values and character were formed. But, of course, the Inavale they saw is not the same Inavale I knew. Only in my quiet recollections does my Inavale still exist. I can never bring my family back to the town where I lived as a girl; but, by remembering and writing, I can bring my Inavale home to them.

Invitation

Evalyn Torrant

Oh, come to my little green garden,
Where daisies bloom bright by the door,
Where pansies peek shyly from baskets,
And day lilies bloom by the score,

Where roses as fragrant as jasmine
Perfume both the day and the night,
Where goldfinches gather at feeders,
Then leave in a twittering flight.

In my garden your troubles, though many
And dark as the shadows at dawn,
Will vanish as quickly as dewdrops
Disperse in the light of the sun.

A Homemaker's Prayer

Louise Weibert Sutton

Lord, let this house be more than walls,
Windowpanes, wide chimneys, and well-rugged floor;
Let there be signs of welcome at the door,
In smiles that greet each visitor who calls;
Let love be as the warmth within its walls
To comfort any person, grieved or poor,
Who enters, friend or stranger, at the door;
Let house be home, wherein Your dear light falls.
From Your blest Spirit, give this place, O Lord,
That peace which worldly treasure cannot buy:
Faith and contentment as shields against the storm,
Bright riches of the soul time cannot harm,
And grace which toil and trouble will not try,
Firm-founded on Thy bedrock of accord.

The entrance to this adobe and redwood house features flowers,
river rocks, and a small statuary. Photograph by Jessie Walker.

Mother

Theresa Helburn

I have praised many loved ones in my song.
    And yet I stand
Before her shrine, to whom all things belong,
    With empty hand.

Perhaps the ripening future holds a time
    For things unsaid;
Not now; men do not celebrate in rhyme
    Their daily bread.

STRENGTH OF CHARACTER MAY BE

ACQUIRED AT WORK, BUT BEAUTY OF

CHARACTER IS LEARNED AT HOME.

THERE THE AFFECTIONS ARE TRAINED.

THERE THE GENTLE LIFE REACHES US,

THE TRUE HEAVEN LIFE.

    —HENRY DRUMMOND

Photograph by Jessie Walker.

MOTHER

Out of a world of mothers—to
think they gave me you!
So loving, kind and thoughtful—
so good, so dear, so true!
And every day this is my prayer:
"God keep you safe and
free from care."

There is in all this cold and hollow world
no fount of deep, strong, deathless love,
save that within a mother's heart.

—Felicia Hemans

Children, look in those eyes, listen to that dear voice, notice the feeling of even a single touch that is bestowed upon you by that gentle hand! Make much of it while yet you have that most precious of all good gifts, a loving mother. Read the unfathomable love of those eyes; the kind anxiety of that tone and look, however slight your pain. In afterlife, you may have friends, fond, dear friends, but never will you have again the inexpressible love and gentleness lavished upon you, which none but a mother bestows.

—Thomas Macaulay

Sunlight penetrates the mist in a hardwood forest in Warren, New Hampshire. Photograph by William H. Johnson.

MY MOTHER

Josephine Rice Creelman

I walk upon the rocky shore;
Her strength is in the ocean's roar.
I glance into the shaded pool;
Her mind is there, so calm and cool.
I hear sweet rippling of the sea;
Naught but her laughter 'tis to me.
I gaze into the starry skies,
And there I see her wondrous eyes.
I look into my inmost mind,
And here her inspiration find.
In all I am and hear and see,
My precious mother is with me.

The sea becomes an ocean of pastels in this painting entitled
A GLORIOUS SUNSET by John Brett (1830–1902).
Image from Fine Art Photographic Library, Ltd., London.

To My Mother

Felicia Hemans

If e'er for human bliss or woe
I feel the sympathetic glow;
If e'er my heart has learn'd to know
The gen'rous wish or pray'r;
Who sow'd the germ, with tender hand?
Who mark'd its infant leaves expand?
My mother's fostering care.

And if one flower of charms refined
May grace the garden of my mind,
'Twas she who nursed it there:
She loved to cherish and adorn
Each blossom of the soil;
To banish every weed and thorn
That oft opposed her toil!

And, oh, if e'er I sighed to claim
The palm, the living palm of fame,
The glowing wreath of praise;
If e'er I've wish'd the glitt'ring stores
That fortune on her fav'rite pours;
'Twas but that wealth and fame, if mine,
Round thee with streaming rays might shine
And gild thy sun-bright days!

Morning sun lights a trail through fields of alpine wildflowers on the
Mazama Ridge in Mount Rainier National Park, Washington.
Photograph by Terry Donnelly/Donnelly Austin Photography.

READERS' REFLECTIONS

Mother's Kitchen

Jimmie Oliver Fleming
Chester, Virginia

I remember those times quite well,
Though it often seems like a dream,
Riding my tricycle in Mother's kitchen
While she daily cooked and cleaned.
She placed food in the wood-burning oven
To cook the proper length of time.
She'd then use her handmade straw broom
To sweep trash along a straight line.
I knew that, while peddling along,
I had better stay out of the way
And never let my red tricycle
Go in areas called "astray."

I traveled a certain path,
So very squeaky and wooden,
While smells of gingerbread danced,
As well as pineapple pudding.
Mother made many recipes in her kitchen,
Yet never wrote them down.
I think she also had one for smiling,
For I rarely saw her frown.
I want the same happiness in my home,
And I will certainly try to do my best.
With memories of Mother's kitchen to help me,
I know I will pass the test.

Love Circle

Karona Drummond
Denton, Texas

I wish that for an hour
Again I could be
Five. Or perhaps four,
Or maybe even three.
I'd crawl up in your lap,
Safe and snug and warm,
And take a little nap
In your loving arms.
But now that I'm grown up,
And now that I'm a mom,
I'll do what time allows
With this dear child of my own.
I'll take him in my lap,
Safe and snug and warm,
And he'll take a little nap
In my loving arms.
Love is like a circle:
We go around the bend;
We grow a little older;
But the love, it never ends.

The Rocking Chair

Samuel L. Bontrager
Lake Wales, Florida

Of the many treasures I hold dear,
None will ever compare
With those precious memories
Of Mother's rocking chair.
Standing by so faithfully,
Its duty was never shirked,
Providing comfort for Mother,
While on and on she worked.
When daytime work was done,
In her rocker she would sit,
Humming familiar tunes
While her hands would deftly knit.
Her chair creaked just slightly,
In harmony with the ticking clock.
Mother would slowly rock away
While darning another sock.
Although Mother is not here today
To render her love and care,
The love will always radiate
With thoughts of her rocking chair.

THROUGH MY WINDOW

Pamela Kennedy

MATERNITY SUIT

It used to be that when you got pregnant, you got to relax. Everyone looked at you with bemused smiles, patted your tummy, and told you to slow down and take care of yourself. You got permission to put away your regular duds and put on roomier ones. Maternity wear was pretty much limited to pants or skirts with elastic panels in the front, tent-shaped tops that demurely covered the "bun in the oven," as my father used to call it, and diaphanous dresses.

No more. As many of my friends are becoming grandmothers, I am being introduced to a whole new world of expectancy. "Maternity fashion," an oxymoron just a few decades ago, is the new big thing. And forget about relaxing. The new trend is to work out and get into shape, not out of it!

Modern expectant mothers don't hide their lights under a bushel either. From business suits to beaches, they let those lights shine with form-fitting frocks and boldly bare midriffs. And this new trend isn't lost on Madison Avenue. Pregnancy today is big business and a whole new industry is out there making the most of it.

One of my friends recently told me that her son and daughter-in-law were expecting their first child, so she wanted to send the mother-to-be a little something to add to her wardrobe. Being a modern "grandma-in-waiting," she went online.

"Do you know there are designers who just create maternity clothes?" she asked me one morning as we took our morning walk. "And they don't specialize in tent tops, either! Oh, no, today it's tight and revealing. A company called Belly Dance offers 'hip maternity clothes,' while From Here to Maternity prefers to call their line 'stylish.' But the crème de la crème of maternity fashions these days

---

It seems all the simple things in life, including pregnancy, have become more complicated.

---

is," she paused dramatically, "A Pea in the Pod."

"Oh, cute," I offered, picturing little cotton prints.

"Well, only if you have a small fortune. This is where all the A-list actresses shop for their maternity clothes. Oh, and no more pajamas," she continued. "It's *ma*jamas now."

It seems all the simple things in life, including pregnancy, have become much more complicated. Today's expectant moms can't relax and just sit around reading novels while growing exponentially. There are whole fitness regimes designed just for them! Pilates and yoga seem to be leading the pack, but there are prenatal aerobics classes too. And I found a quote from a reproductive biologist who said he knows women who have completed marathons, triathlons, and even cross-country ski races while pregnant!

Whatever happened to the idea of taking a break in preparation for the upcoming eighteen-plus years of child rearing, of seeing pregnancy as the calm before the storm?

Today's moms-in-waiting are not only being pressured to be pregnant fashion plates, however. They also have the added burden of getting a head start on their child's intellectual development! This year, one of the top-selling gifts for expectant mothers is a deluxe kit containing a prenatal heart listener with two headsets, a CD of classical music, a maternity belt, fetal microphone, and dual speaker set. With this nifty little kit you can, as the ad proclaims joyfully, "Listen, talk, and play music to your unborn baby!" The illustration on the front of this "perfect gift" shows a rapturous mom and dad (in headsets) speaking into a microphone strapped to the mother's belly. I'm sure "prenatal classics" were playing in the background.

This, frankly, scares me. The kid isn't even born yet and she's getting instructions from her overachieving parents—set to Beethoven! While it does offer the appeal of being able to talk to your child without having her sass back, personally I think this is a trend that needs to be reined in.

Even at my age, I still vividly recall those days of waiting for my children to be born. They were long days, especially the summer ones, filled with swollen ankles and a tired back. I didn't feel particularly enthused about fashion or exercise, and especially enjoyed just daydreaming about what it would be like to have a healthy baby and a waist again. In my book, pregnant mommies are the ones who need to be cuddled and loved and listened to. They need to be free to wear over-sized T-shirts and baggy pants without any fashionistas telling them to squeeze into a camisole and "let it all hang out." They should be the ones listening to the classics—heaven knows, there won't be much serenity once that baby arrives.

And if they want to take a walk or go to an exercise class, I think that's great; but let's give them permission to put their feet up now and then and order out for pizza or pickles or Rocky Road hot-fudge sundaes. Pretty soon, the pea will be out of the pod—and then, all bets are off!

Pamela Kennedy writes short stories, articles, essays, and children's books. She resides in Honolulu, Hawaii, with her husband, a retired naval officer. They have three adult children.

Original artwork by Doris Ettlinger.

FOR THE CHILDREN

Nap

Eileen Spinelli

Such a busy day for me—
watching squirrels
    race round a tree,
waving at
    the big red truck,
splashing with
    my rubber duck,
prancing
    wearing Daddy's hat,
dancing with
    the kitty cat,
helping Auntie
    stir and cook,
coloring
    my bunny book,
building bridges,
    roads, and farms.

Time to rest in
Mommy's arms,
    take a cozy nap,
    and then—
off I'll go
to play again.

Original artwork by Russ Flint.

Little Moments

Melissa Lester

THE BIG EVENTS OF FAMILY LIFE—holidays, vacations, and birthdays—are documented in volumes of photo albums Mother carefully organized, but many of my fondest memories of growing up are found in the images of daily life that fill my mind.

Sunday was an important day for our family. Church was the central focus of our family life, and I still remember the preparations Mother made to ready the family for worship. She often rolled my hair on Saturday night. We would watch *Little House on the Prairie* or talk about "girl stuff" as she brushed each section of hair and twisted it into a curler. This was a small ritual, of course, but when I longed to have a daughter of my own, one of the first images that would come to my mind was snuggling up on my bed to roll her hair in pink sponge curlers.

Even the most mundane tasks of daily living seem more significant in retrospect. I remember one particular bath time when my five-year-old heart was burdened. Guilt overwhelmed me as I cried, admitting that I had been paddled in kindergarten that day for talking during naptime. Always a worrier, I was certain my once-spotless record of conduct was ruined forever. Mother assured me that all was not lost. As she bathed me that night, she tenderly washed the scarlet letter of shame away.

She reminded me that each new day provided an opportunity to begin anew, and I emerged from that bath feeling clean and hopeful again.

These little moments of caretaking that filled Mother's day showed me that I was not just taken care *of*, but also cared *for*. Because of her love, my teeth were brushed, my hair was combed, and I had vitamins to take.

Mother made me feel special in myriad ways. I looked forward to the end of each school day, knowing Mother would have ready a cup of hot chocolate in my favorite "Raggedy Ann" mug. I would tell her about the ups and downs of life in elementary school as I sipped the rich, warm cocoa, savoring the marshmallows she had sprinkled on top.

On days she was called to pick me up early because of illness, I would arrive home to find the covers already turned back on my bed and a favorite gown spread out on the pillow. While I snuggled cozily under the covers, Mother would make Welsh rarebit, a cheesy white sauce she would pour over soda crackers. Even though its appeal is lost on our spouses today, my sister, brother, and I still think of Welsh rarebit as the ultimate comfort food.

Although Mother often told me she loved me, her acts of nurturing spoke more eloquently than her words. Each time she rubbed my hand during church, hugged me when I came home

*Beautifully decorated desserts are presented on a hand-painted tabletop
and chairs in a garden setting. Photograph by Jessie Walker.*

from school, or kissed me good night, she left a lasting impression on my heart.

Many of my happiest moments were times when Mother paused to have fun with me. Once, she draped a sheet over the kitchen table and we crawled underneath. What a magical time this was for a four-year-old, drinking invisible tea with Mommy in our secret castle!

We also spent time together cooking. I still have the preschool cookbook with a recipe for peanut-butter balls. In our earliest days of making the cookies, I dutifully rolled the gooey dough into balls as suggested. As my baking confidence grew, we progressed to pressing a Hershey's Kiss into each ball or imprinting the cookies with a fork.

Years later, I was shaping the cookies into letters, teddy bears, and holiday designs. Little moments of playfulness helped me understand

that Mother not only loved me, but she liked me too. I felt special knowing that out of all the people in the world, I was one of her favorites.

Now that I am a mother myself, memories remind me of the importance of day-to-day activities in filling our home with love. Each time I run the children's bath water, snuggle up with one who is feeling sick, or call them all to the kitchen to make our favorite peanut-butter pie recipe, I am reminded that these little moments will add up to a lifetime of love. Pieced together, little moments with Mother work together like a patchwork quilt to keep us feeling secure, knowing we will always be wrapped in our mother's love.

Melissa Lester, a frequent contributor to IDEALS, *is the author of a Bible study book for women; she is also a professional conference speaker. She and her family live in Alabama.*

Day Dreams

Margaret Johnson

I measured myself by the wall in the garden;
The hollyhocks blossomed far over my head.
"Oh, when I can touch with the tips of my fingers
The highest green bud, with its lining of red,

"I shall not be a child anymore, but a woman.
Dear hollyhock blossoms, how glad I shall be!
I wish they would hurry—the years that are coming—
And bring the bright days that I dream of to me!

"Oh, when I am grown, I shall know all my lessons;
There's so much to learn when one's only just ten!
I shall be very rich, very handsome, and stately,
And good, too, of course—'twill be easier then!

"There'll be many to love me, and nothing to vex me,
No knots in my sewing; no crusts to my bread.
My days will go by like the days in a story,
The sweetest and gladdest that ever was read.

"And then I shall come out some day to the garden
(For this little corner must always be mine);
I shall wear a white gown, all embroidered with silver,
That trails in the grass with a rustle and shine.

"And, meeting some child here at play in the sunshine,
With gracious hands laid on her head, I shall say,
'I measured myself by these hollyhock blossoms
When I was no taller than you, dear, one day!'

"She will smile in my face as I stoop low to kiss her,
And—Hark! they are calling me in to my tea!
O blossoms, I wish that the slow years would hurry!
When, when will they bring all I dream of to me?"

*Yellow hollyhocks are the centerpiece of the arrangement in this painting entitled
A STILL LIFE OF HOLLYHOCKS AND NASTURTIUM by Antoinine Berjon. Image from
Fine Art Photographic Library, Ltd., London/John Mitchell & Son, London.*

Psalms by Lamplight

Geraldine Ross

Above the bread, the china cup,
Believing, patient eyes look up.
They lift themselves unto the hills
Beyond the plant-filled window sills;
They catch, they hold the light like grace;
Light overflows the heart, the face,
And in a burst of glory, shines
On fingers tracing cherished lines:
"I shall not want." No doubt nor grief
Darkens this radiant belief.
The ceiling shelters like a wing
Where Mother and a kettle sing.

*The woman who creates and sustains a home, and
under whose hands children grow up to be strong and
pure men and women, is a creator second only to God.*

—Helen Maria Fiske Hunt Jackson

*Lilacs spilling out of an antique vase freshen the table.
Photograph by William H. Johnson.*

SOMEONE TO REMEMBER

Connie Wetzell

HER GIFT

When I was a girl, I always hurried home from school on Wednesdays. The familiar aroma of garlic blended with crushed tomatoes and fresh basil would greet me as I walked through the door of our home on the south side of Chicago. Then I would head straight to the kitchen to find Ma. I can still see her standing at the stove, stirring the spaghetti sauce in my grandmother's old metal pot. She was beautiful, with her brown eyes smiling at me and her thick, dark brown hair tucked behind her ears. From the hi-fi came the sounds of one of her favorite singers—maybe Connie Francis, Frank Sinatra, or Dean Martin. For Ma, music and cooking went hand in hand.

Only after I greeted her with a kiss would Ma stop stirring and put down her big wooden spoon long enough to pull off a piece of bread from a warm loaf. She would hand me the bread and say, "Go ahead, Baby, *mangia*," which seems to be every Italian mother's favorite word—"Eat!" I would happily dip the warm bread into the sauce and have a taste, just enough to whet my appetite for the Wednesday-night dinner of pasta, meatballs, and sausage that would soon follow. That was my life growing up in an Italian family: music playing, food cooking, and, at the center of it all, Ma.

Ma was a stay-at-home mother, and her life consisted of "doing" for her family. She was there for singing lessons, dance classes, play auditions, Little League ball, and every other activity. Ma was fiercely proud of my sister, my brother, and me, and our talents and accomplishments. "You gotta hear my daughter sing," she would say, as I cringed self-consciously. And then, kissing her fingers, she would announce, "She's got a beautiful voice!"

While publicly I may have cringed at her effusive praise, inside I treasured it. My mother had a wonderful way with children; we felt so certain of her love that we grew up to believe anything was within our reach. Ma was always there to encourage me, to pray with me, and to build

---

That was my life growing up in an Italian family: music playing, food cooking, and, at the center of it all, Ma.

---

me up. When times were hard, she never failed to make me see that there would be brighter days ahead. Ma was a woman of great faith. "Don't worry, Honey," she'd say, "God has everything under control." Her optimism was contagious. With Ma believing in me so fiercely, I had no choice but to believe in myself.

And Ma's gift with children extended beyond her own three. She welcomed all my friends with open arms, a kiss on both cheeks, and, of course, plenty of food. In college, I spent a summer touring the country with a singing group. When the tour passed close to Chicago, I wanted to bring my friends home to meet Ma. Giving her just a single day's notice, I called and asked her to cook a big Italian feast for all eighteen of us. Without hesitation, she replied, "Sure, Doll, what time can I expect you?" Ma cooked a traditional Italian meal, with several courses of pasta, meat, potatoes, vegetables, and more. She served my father first, as she did at every meal, and then sent the rest of us through a buffet line and into the family room to find a place to sit and eat. Ma made each one of my friends feel welcome; they all left that night full of her wonderful food and touched by her spirit and warmth.

Last year, the day after my younger daughter's wedding, I was the one cooking the Italian feast—sauce, meatballs, sausage, salad, and tomato bread—for three generations of my family. As we all sat around the dining-room table talking, I looked at Ma. Her complexion was still so beautiful and her hair still shone a rich dark brown. As she took her first bite, I anxiously awaited her reaction. She winked at me and said, "Delicious. Tastes just like mine." Another gift from Ma.

I am blessed by two daughters who have grown up to be very much like their grandmother. They both love music and cooking, and both have chosen jobs that allow their grandmother's faith and her giving nature to shine through—one works with the elderly and the other teaches children with disabilities.

One recent night, after falling asleep fretting about one of my girls, I had a dream that I spoke to Ma. "What's Jesus like?" I asked her. "He's good with children," was her reply. This answer seemed strange at first, but then I understood. Now that she has gone, Ma has finally passed the job of caring for her children on to Him.

Connie Wetzell is an award-winning radio personality and a voice-over artist, as well as an inspirational conference speaker and an author.

Photograph by Jessie Walker.

SLICE OF LIFE

Edna Jaques

THESE THINGS ARE GOOD

To give a little homeless child a home,
 A piece of silver in a beggar's hand,
A load of wood to the old, helpless poor,
 The sound of rain upon a thirsty land;

To comfort people who are sore oppressed,
 And love your neighbor with a kindly grace;
To speak to strangers when they come to church,
 And show the world a cheerful smiling face;

These things are good: the smell of cedar trees,
 Lupines as blue as heaven in a field,
The drift of smoke, the flame of yellow broom,
 A scarred old tree whose broken bark has healed,

White snow to hide the shivering fields from sight,
 Blue shadows in the folds of a ravine,
A little gilt-edged card with Christmas trees,
 A frozen pond where silver willows lean.

For all good things abide: the fir trees growing,
 A love of home and fires in a grate,
A lighted doorway and a table set,
 And mother watching for us at the gate.

An Optimist's Promise

Betty Dubecki Hochstrasser

A raindrop fell upon my lip.
I licked it off to see if it
Would taste like honey,
    As my mother said it would.

A snowflake lit upon my sleeve.
I watched it closely to perceive
It glisten like an angel's wing,
    As my mother said it would.

A ray of sunshine sparked my tears.
I wondered then if it appeared
To shimmer smiles through to me,
    As my mother said it would.

Now, raindrops on my tongue are sweet,
The snowflakes' message, clear,
And sunshine laughs out loud with me,
    As my mother's always near.

An azalea hedge is a beautiful part of this South Carolina garden at Brookgreen Gardens in Murrells Inlet. Photograph by William H. Johnson.

Inset: Catawba rhododendron is touched by dew. Photograph by William H. Johnson.

My Mother's Love

Virginia Wave McPheeters

There is no other love so tender,
There is no hand so gentle and kind,
There is no heart so understanding,
As that dear, sweet mother of mine.

No matter that life rushes onward,
That things seem ever to change;
No matter the time or the distance,
My mother's love is the same.

Whenever the way seems lonely,
When burdens are heavy to bear,
My heart finds solace and comfort
Remembering my mother's care.

Her own special care still surrounds me,
Though she now lives in heaven above;
Each day my heart finds a blessing
Through my mother's great gift of love.

Legacy

Mary Carlier

My mother left me lovely things:
The orisons of birds,
The hushed soliloquies of leaves,
The silent peace of herds.

She willed me gossamers of song
And taught me when to pray;
She had the courage—tranquil, sure—
That I could use today.

But, oh, the gift I cherish most
In all her legacy—
The depth of love she had, to give
His mother's name to me.

*The Blue Ridge Mountains are framed by a young hickory tree in Shenandoah National Park, Virginia.
Photograph by Terry Donnelly/Donnelly Austin Photography.*

Mother

My mother was the making of me. She was so true and so sure of me, I felt that I had someone to live for—someone I must not disappoint. The memory of my mother will always be a blessing to me.

— Thomas Edison

I shall never forget my mother, for it was she who planted and nurtured the first seeds of good within me. She opened my heart to the lasting impressions of nature; she awakened my understanding and extended my horizon, and her precepts exerted an everlasting influence upon the course of my life.

— Immanuel Kant

Fifty-four years of love and tenderness and crossness and devotion and unswerving loyalty. Without [Mother] I could have achieved a quarter of what I have achieved, not only in terms of success and career, but in terms of personal happiness. . . . She has never stood between me and my life, never tried to hold me too tightly, always let me go free. . . .

— Noel Coward

Evening light bathes the Tatoosh Range in Mount Rainier National Park, Washington. Photograph by Terry Donnelly/Donnelly Austin Photography.

The Gift of Giggles

Vicky L. Crager

I grew up on a small farm with a shortage of worldly goods. Thanks to Mother, we were so rich in enthusiasm and stubbornness and love, I did not miss the other things.

Like most Americans, my ancestry is a mixture of several cultures. Many of my forebears were stern, hard-working Swiss and determined, hard-working English people. Somewhere back in the great-greats, one of my grandfathers had the good sense to marry a dark-haired, laughing French woman. Her passion added hope to determination and a zing to hard work. Since her addition to my family tree, occasionally a dark-haired, laughing baby has popped up. I am fortunate that one such baby became my mother. My father thrived alongside her laughter and openness. We all did.

I am of the stern Swiss persuasion and so was my father. One time when I was feeling scornful of Mother laughing with her sister over some silliness, Dad confided that he loved my mother because she knew how to giggle. I was astonished, but since then I have come to appreciate my father's wisdom.

Our white farmhouse was small; the girls' bedroom shared a wall with my parents' room.

One of my earliest memories is being lullabied to sleep by my parents' quiet laughter and talk of dreams.

We had playhouses scattered over the farm: a big pine with branches sweeping the ground, a corner of the woodshed, or just simple "rooms" outlined by boards and tree trunks. Mother inspected our work on these playhouses with a wonder approaching awe. Her praises were what we worked so hard to hear.

Our favorite playhouse was an abandoned woodshed. We hauled out many years' worth of accumulated wood shavings with an old bucket. Mother climbed the hill to encourage us whenever she could slip away from household responsibilities. When we finished decorating the swept-clean woodshed, she brought us a play dinner to celebrate, then marveled over every contrived piece of furniture.

Our playhouses were hobbies; the work around the farm was not. My grandmother, who lived with us, would tell me I might as well learn to enjoy working because that was what life was all about. I did not accept her advice easily. I did not like farm work. Feeding the animals was a daily torment; washing milkers and cleaning the barn were burdens.

The worst time of year was haying season. While my friends went on vacations to exotic places, I hauled hay. Discomfort was too mild a word for what I felt when rolling bales, helping unload, or nursing haycuts. I complained as much as I dared, which was not much, and made solemn vows never to live on a farm when I grew up.

As the years passed, however, I finally noticed some things that changed my mind about work, especially hauling hay.

Mother and Dad enjoyed what they were doing; there was a deep, urgent pleasure in clearing a good crop of hay, stacking it in the barn, preparing for winter. There was satisfaction in nurturing a calf and having it respond to the sight of me. There was also a camaraderie—when I was not trying to get out of work.

Mother was the spiritual center of these revelations, Dad was the physical. Mother was small, so my father would not let her do much heavy work. But she was in the fields as often as small children and household chores would permit, her laughter punctuating our chores. We had wonderful picnics on the "back forty," acreage we owned away from the main farm, while Dad was mowing or raking or baling. Mother always had a cool drink, accompanied by a smile, to greet us when we came in to unload hay. In the winter, we had hot meals on cold nights after the chores were done. Jokes and fairy tales, along with giggles, were tucked into the cracks of work-long days.

I often think of my childhood as I raise children of my own. Even though I do not play and laugh with the spontaneity of my mother, because of rich memories I am not as grim as my natural tendencies could lead me to be. Remembering her open delight in sunrises or playhouses helps me express joy to my own family. My father knew what he was doing when he married Mother because she had the gift of giggles.

A good laugh
is sunshine
in a house.

—William Makepeace Thackeray

BITS & PIECES

Into the woman's keeping is committed the destiny of the generations to come after us.
—*Theodore Roosevelt*

No language can express the power and beauty and heroism and majesty of a mother's love.
—*Edwin H. Chapin*

Nature's loving proxy, the watchful mother.
—*Edward George Earle Bulwer-Lytton*

I think my life began with waking up and loving my mother's face.
—*George Eliot*

If there be aught surpassing human deed or word or thought, it is a mother's love!
—*Marchioness de Spadara*

The dignity, the grandeur, the tenderness, the everlasting and divine significance of motherhood . . . .
—*De Witt Talmage*

Sometimes the laughter in mothering is the recognition of the ironies and absurdities. Sometimes, though, it's just pure, unthinking delight.

—*Barbara Schapiro*

And so, my love, my mother,
I shall always be true to you. . . .

—*D. H. Lawrence*

Mothers have as powerful an influence over the welfare of future generations as all other causes combined.

—*John Abbot*

Say to mothers, what a holy charge is theirs, with what a kingly power their love might rule the fountains of the newborn mind.

—*Lydia H. Sigourney*

The doctors told me that I would never walk; but my mother told me I would, so I believed my mother.

—*Wilma Rudolph*

My Mother's Garden

George Nicholas Rees

My mother hastened in the spring
To sow petunia beds;
She planted coxcomb, quick to bring
A host of feath'ry heads;
She sought to cherish every thing
That brightened old homesteads.

My mother liked to fuss a bit
About her favorite flowers.
Ofttimes she chose to sit and knit
Through summer twilight hours;
She marked each moth that chanced to flit
Around these fragrant bowers.

Her hollyhocks had giant stalks;
The cannas grew so tall;
Primroses thrived along the walks;
Shrubs hid the garden wall.
Her garden was the kind that talks
From early spring till fall.

A profusion of pink roses bending
ragged in the rain speaks to me of
all gentleness and its enduring.
— William Carlos Williams

Opposite: This hybrid tea rose, named Miss All-American Beauty, is also known as the Maria Callas rose and has a wonderful fragrance. Photograph by LeFever/Grushow/Grant Heilman.

Overleaf: This garden walk is arrayed with the beauty of spring. Photograph by William H. Johnson.

COUNTRY CHRONICLE

Lansing Christman

FRIEND TO A SONG SPARROW

Years ago, my wife, Lucile, made friends with a song sparrow.

It was May. Orioles were back in the elms, and the creek by the house was singing in murmuring, purling tunes. There were ample bushes and shrubs around the yard—lilac, honeysuckle, and forsythia. There were hedges. Why would this song sparrow choose a site on the ground to build its nest, just a few steps from our door?

The bird became so familiar with Lucile's footsteps that she could, with patience and gentleness, reach down and stroke the crown of the sparrow while it sat quietly on the nest. The only response was a calm blink of the eyes. The procedure required affection and gentleness, and Lucile would speak softly as she approached. The result was a priceless dividend, a trusting friendship between a housewife and a dooryard song sparrow.

I was late that year in bringing out the mower. Grass grew lush and tall.

This spring, I hope a sparrow is singing its song from a nearby bush or thicket. And I hope it is a descendant of the one by the doorstep that grew to trust Lucile's tender touch.

The author of four books, Lansing Christman has contributed to IDEALS *for more than thirty years. Mr. Christman has also been published in several American, international, and Braille anthologies. He lives in rural South Carolina.*

This front porch in Peachum, Vermont, welcomes visitors to sit and stay awhile. Photograph by Dianne Dietrich Leis/Dietrich Leis Stock Photography.

53

Mother Love

Katherine Edelman

Of all the love that has been known
Since time and earth began,
Of all the faith that has been shown
Since God created man,
Of all the noble, stirring deeds
That grace the written page,
A mother's love and faith and hope
Stand out through every age.

Her deeds have moved a careless world
To pity and to tears;
Her love has kindled faith and trust
Through all the changing years;
Her selflessness and sacrifice,
Her faith through praise or blame
Have enshrined her in the hearts of all
And glorified her name.

For though a world may frown or sneer
And failure mark the hours,
Her reaching love encircles us,
A rosary of flowers;
A shining chain so sweet with blooms
Of prayer and love and trust,
It touches with a heavenly light
Our weak and mortal dust.

This home garden abounds with zinnias, lilies, loosestrife, yarrow, marigolds, and other flowers. Photograph by Alan and Linda Detrick/Grant Heilman.

BACKYARD CALENDAR

Joan Donaldson

SCATTERING SUNSHINE

Carrying a basket, I slip into my garden. Sunlight falls upon the rabbit tracks that dance across the freshly tilled soil between my onion rows. I forgot to close the wooden gate yesterday, and a family of bunnies born underneath a nearby viola have evidently been back for a visit. The mother rabbit took her brood away from my garden once they were old enough to venture into the broader world, but I suppose last night they sniffed the opportunity to sample my young vegetable plants and could not resist a return visit to their first home.

I wander through the beds, following the rabbit tracks and inspecting the peas, carrots, and broccoli. A few nibbles of beet tops and a bite from the outer leaves of the cabbage are the only noticeable damage. Even rabbits do not touch the tender shoots rising from the roses along the wooden garden fence. Their tracks also avoid the garlic bed. Not me. I brush the gray-green blades to fill the air with the intense aroma that makes me look forward to mounds of pesto heaped onto fresh bread. At the end of one of my garlic rows I find a half-chewed daffodil. I cup the flower in my hand and wonder why the rabbits selected this beauty to nibble.

While I try to be orderly in the vegetable garden and place onion sets and garlic cloves in straight rows, I prefer to scatter spring bulbs like patches of sunshine. Golden trumpets sparkle near the garden gate, and outside of the fence a clump of daffodils floats a sweet fragrance into the air. In front of the garden shed, blue scilla freckle the lawn, their small bells bobbing in the breeze.

When my sons were small, planting bulbs was a fall family ritual that produced flowers for

The perfume of apple blossoms drifts from the tree overhanging my fence.

May Day baskets and Mother's Day bouquets. I would give each boy a paper bag filled with tulip, crocus, and daffodil bulbs. Then, miniature orange shovels in hand, the brothers would set off with their father. While I dug holes in the flowerbeds next to the house, John and the boys, like squirrels readying for winter, buried bulbs all over the yard. In spring, I would discover purple crocus near the picnic table, or snowdrops under the clothesline, or yellow jonquils nodding along the driveway. As our sons grew older, their plantings spread farther across our farm. Now when I gaze beyond my garden fence, I see hundreds of daffodils twinkle around the outbuildings and on the hill facing our home.

On this particular Mother's Day, neither of

our sons is able to return home. But Carlos, my younger son, visited a week ago. He rattled up the driveway in his red pickup truck and presented me with a hanging basket overflowing with bright pink petunias. Carlos tends his own garden now, and our visits are often full of talk of what to plant and how to care for his rose bushes. His gift basket, swinging beside our door, is a cheerful reminder of our shared passion for growing things.

My own mother grew up on a farm and tells stories of playing in the orchards during blossom time. Like the mother rabbit that nurtured her family under a viola, she taught me to love flowers as soon as I could follow her through our backyard. Now that her garden is reduced to a small plot, I like to return her gift with bouquets from my own yard. Most of the buds on our apple tree have opened; bees dart through the pink and sage-green haze, and purple violets bloom beneath the tree. I snip sprays of apple blossoms for a Mother's Day bouquet, hopeful

> *Like the mother rabbit that nurtured her family under a viola, my mother taught me to love flowers as soon as I could follow her through our backyard.*

that their fragrance will bring my mother happy thoughts.

I place the apple blossoms and the shears in my basket and check that the garden gate is securely latched. I understand the mother rabbit's desire to share my garden with her young ones; but for today at least, I would rather they feasted on the wildflowers blooming outside the garden fence.

Joan Donaldson is the author of books for children and young adults, as well as essays that have appeared in national publications. She and her husband raised their sons on Pleasant Hill Farm in Michigan, where they continue to practice rural skills.

Original artwork by Stacy Venturi-Pickett.

Mother's Heart

Thelma Allinder

Her white spireas carried bridal sprays,
And Japanese quince flaunted flaming hue;
Pink flowering almonds, with their gracious ways,
Greeted the mellowing sunshine anew.
Old-fashioned lilacs, adorned with mauve plumes,
Lured butterfly and small bee to full banquets there;
June roses mingled scent with rare perfumes
Of flowers vivid and shyly fair.
Petunias and bright-skirted hollyhocks,
The vari-colored moss, and golden glow
Were as welcomed as the gayly petaled phlox,
The zinnias, and the moon-pale mountain snow.
Our home was circled by a rich paradise
Because my mother's heart was garden-wise.

Beneath these fruit-tree boughs that shed
Their snow-white blossoms on my head,
With brightest sunshine round me spread
Of spring's unclouded weather,
In this sequestered nook, how sweet
To sit upon my orchard-seat!
And birds and flowers once more to greet,
My last year's friends together.
—William Wordsworth

White multi-flora roses grace the banks of the Guinea Brook in Sharon, Connecticut. Photograph by William H. Johnson.

I Think of My Mother

Jessie Cannon Eldridge

I think of my mother in a garden.
She was a farmer's daughter. She knew
The touch of the earth and the way
Each plant grew.
Emerald peppers, ruby tomatoes,
Amethyst grapes on the vine . . .
These were her jewels, these were her treasures,
Lovely, fine.
I think of my mother in a garden:
Easter lilies, lilacs, phlox,
Blue violets, and portulaca
By our walks.
I think of my mother in a garden,
Loving it always, turning the sod—
My mother, farmer's daughter,
Eve, woman of God.

More than anything, I must have flowers, always, always.
— Claude Monet

This comfortable garden room offers a nice respite from everyday life. Photograph by Jessie Walker.

Faith

John Banister Tabb

In every seed to breathe a flower,
In every drop of dew
To reverence a cloistered star
Within the distant blue;
To wait the promise of the bow,
Despite the cloud between,
Is faith—the fervid evidence
Of loveliness unseen.

The best and most beautiful things in the

world cannot be seen or even touched.

They must be felt with the heart.

—Helen Keller

Wildflowers adorn the fields for everyone to enjoy.
Photograph by Larry LeFever/Grant Heilman.

Ageless Motherhood

Grace Noll Crowell

Our tongue holds many vital words,
But among them is no other
As meaningful and beautiful
As the precious name of *Mother*.

A name brimful of selfless love,
So fraught with gracious living,
So swift with its outpouring wealth
Of sacrificial giving.

And yet beyond these splendid gifts
Are the memories she is making
In loved ones' hearts: a kitchen's scent
Of wholesome, home-sweet baking;

Of a table simply, neatly spread
With food of her preparing;
Her healing touch, her gentle voice
That tells of constant caring.

Oh, all of life's essential things
She always shares with others,
The simple joys of every day,
That wealth of all true mothers.

*A new baby is introduced into the family in the painting
entitled THE INTRODUCTION by Emily Crawford (circa
1869–1900). Image from Fine Art Photographic Library,
Ltd., London/Fine Art of Oakham.*

Mother's Measuring Cup

Vivian Marie Chatman

A crystal cup for measuring,
As baking day rolled by,
And all the sweet ingredients
For spicy cake or pie
Were kept on Mother's cupboard shelf.
The cup held generosity
Accepted with delight
On lovely little luncheon trays
And grand desserts at night.
A measure of her brimming cup
Of eagerness to please,
Her cup of heartfelt kindness
Made our sweetest memories.

A bent-willow porch swing decorates a porch in Lake Oswego, Oregon. Photograph by Dianne Dietrich Leis/Dietrich Leis Stock Photography.

FROM AMERICA'S ATTIC

D. Fran Morley

ROASTED, PERKED, AND SIPPED

Coffee has been the world's social beverage since the sixth century, when Ethiopians first discovered its appealing flavor. From there, a taste for coffee spread throughout the Arab world. By the 1600s, coffee had arrived in western Europe and England, where coffeehouses arose as the place for intellectuals to gather to discuss the events of the day.

European settlers brought their love of coffee with them to North America: as early as 1689, coffeehouses were operating in Boston, New York, and Philadelphia. Coffee even played a symbolic role in the birth of the American nation. Those who planned the 1773 Boston Tea Party, according to legend, met in a coffeehouse to formulate their revolt against King George's infamous tea tax. And in that same year, the Continental Congress declared coffee the "official national beverage." What better way for the new country to turn its back on England than by pledging allegiance to an alternative to Great Britain's beloved tea.

As the new nation expanded, its love of coffee grew. In the American West, settlers and cowboys made a simple brew by pouring ground coffee into a pot of water and bringing the mixture to a rolling boil. After the pot was set off the heat for a few minutes so that the grounds would settle, the hot, strong brew was ready to drink. Today's coffee connoisseurs might consider this type of brew a travesty; indeed, it calls up images of coffee so strong that a spoon can stand upright in a cup. But it was likely this type of coffee that Mark Twain was describing when he wrote, "after a few months' acquaintance with European 'coffee,' one's mind weakens, and his faith with it,

---

Not all coffee drinkers were satisfied with the thick, strong brew Twain loved, however; the quest for a perfect cup of coffee has led to many new and inventive ways of brewing.

---

and he begins to wonder if the rich beverage of home, with its clotted layer of yellow cream on top of it, is not a mere dream after all and a thing which never existed."

Not all coffee drinkers were satisfied with the thick, strong brew Twain loved; the quest for a perfect cup of coffee has led to many new and inventive ways of brewing. Those who preferred a slightly more delicate flavor began filtering the coffee grounds using metal screens or cloth bags. The coffee was then allowed to steep to the desired strength. In 1912, an ingenious German woman invented paper filters, the forerunners of those we still use today.

Brewing coffee became an easier task with

the introduction of the percolator. Around the turn of the twentieth century, the percolator worked its way into American kitchens, along with other such brewing systems as the French Press Pot and the glass vacuum pot. However, most American adults fondly remember the percolator merrily bubbling on the stovetop, brewing coffee for breakfast, lunch, and dinner. As coffee became easier to brew at home, a variety of coffee brands began to appear on grocery shelves.

Coffee, now firmly entrenched as a part of American home life, invaded the workplace. The phrase "take a coffee break" may imply a respite from labor, but employers actually had more, rather than less work on their minds when the official coffee break was initiated. Employers had begun to note that coffee appeared to stimulate afternoon production levels. Some accounts credit a soap manufacturer in New York as the first to offer workers coffee in 1901; others state it was the Mississippi Steamboat Company in New Orleans in 1930.

Civilian employers, however, were a few steps behind the U.S. military, which had long understood the value of coffee to its soldiers. During the Civil War, the federal government supplied Union soldiers with a yearly ration of thirty-six pounds of coffee. World War I soldiers were supplied with a new kind of coffee—instant. When the soldiers returned home, they brought with them a taste for this easy-to-prepare beverage.

Today, coffeehouses seem to stand at every corner in our modern cities. Even though they offer

This May 1923 advertisement in THE LADIES HOME JOURNAL states that "years add only honor to the worthy." Image used with permission from KF Holdings.

lengthy menus, they are not really that different from the coffeehouses of seventeenth-century New England. Now, as then, they lure us in with the simple, irresistible promise of a place to sit, relax, and talk over a steaming-hot cup of our favorite brew. The declaration of the Continental Congress still holds true—coffee is, without a doubt, our national drink. It begins our days, fuels our workplaces, and bonds our friendships.

Fran Morley is a freelance writer and a former editor of IDEALS. She and her husband live in Alabama.

FAMILY RECIPES

The wonderful bounty of summer vegetables provides many opportunities for delicious dinners. Enjoy these favorite vegetable recipes from our readers.

TASTY CARROTS

Phyllis M. Peters, Three Rivers, Michigan

1 pound carrots, cooked
3 tablespoons butter, melted
1 tablespoon prepared horseradish
¼ teaspoon garlic powder
¼ teaspoon salt

In a small bowl, combine butter, horseradish, garlic powder, and salt; mix well. Place hot carrots in serving dish. Add butter mixture and stir until carrots are evenly coated. Makes 4 servings.

CAULIFLOWER AND BROCCOLI CASSEROLE

Alba DiPaola, Williamsville, New York

1 head cauliflower
1 head broccoli
1 tablespoon olive oil
⅛ teaspoon garlic powder
¼ teaspoon lemon basil
¼ teaspoon salt
½ cup Mozzarella cheese, shredded
½ cup Sharp Cheddar cheese, shredded

Preheat oven to 300°F. Break cauliflower and broccoli into flowerets. In a large saucepan, cook vegetables until tender. Drain and place in a 7- x 11-inch baking dish. In a small bowl, combine olive oil, garlic powder, basil, and salt. Pour over casserole. Sprinkle cheeses over vegetables. Bake 40 minutes, uncovered. Makes 6 servings.

FANCY MASHED POTATOES

Kristi Hellmuth, Alexandria, Virginia

¼ cup milk
8 tablespoons butter, divided
8 russet potatoes, peeled, boiled, and mashed
1 cup sour cream
1 8-ounce package cream cheese
1 teaspoon salt
1 teaspoon seasoned salt

Preheat oven to 325°F. Grease a 9- x 12-inch baking dish. In a small saucepan, warm milk and 2 tablespoons butter until butter is melted. In a large mixing bowl, combine potatoes and milk mixture. Stir sour cream into potatoes and milk; mix well. Break cream cheese into large pieces and add, one at a time, to potato mixture, beating well after each addition. Add salt. Pour potato mixture into baking dish and sprinkle with seasoned salt. Divide remaining butter into pats and place on top of potatoes. (Potatoes may be refrigerated for up to 2 days prior to baking.) Bake 25 minutes, or until edges are browned. Makes 8 servings.

SWEET POTATO CASSEROLE

Nettie Lee Farmer, Crockett, Virginia

3 cups mashed sweet potatoes
1 cup granulated sugar
½ cup butter, divided in half and melted
½ cup milk
1 cup coconut
2 eggs, beaten
1 teaspoon vanilla
1 cup brown sugar
⅓ cup all-purpose flour
1 cup pecans, chopped

Preheat oven to 350°F. In a large bowl, combine hot potatoes with granulated sugar, ¼ cup butter, milk, and coconut. Add eggs and vanilla. Pour into a 9- x 12-inch baking dish. Set aside. In a medium bowl, combine ¼ cup butter with brown sugar. In a small bowl, combine flour with pecans; add to brown sugar mixture. Sprinkle over top of potatoes. Bake 30 minutes. Makes 8 servings.

Grandmother's Pies

Ruth B. Field

Grandmother's pies were not the dainty chiffon concoctions nor lattice-covered delicacies we make today. Her pies were—well, sturdy seems a good word to describe them.

In 1870, my grandmother went as a bride to live in a little valley on Mount Crescent in New Hampshire. My grandfather had built a snug house in this part of the White Mountain Region.

Grandmother was a brisk, small woman who spanked butter vigorously, quoted the Bible to fit any occasion, and sang "Rock-a-Bye Baby" in a way that could lull even the most fretful child to sleep. I remember the low rooms of that old farmhouse as a haven of peace and happiness.

The "setting room" was an entrancing place, with its table topped with a china lamp, its horsehair chair, and its mellow-toned parlor organ with a red stool. Most intriguing of all, I think, was the long mantel which held Grandmother's pink china clock, a small Bisque figurine, some luster cups, and two lovely vases.

But life in the house centered about the kitchen. How well I still remember the pump by the sink, which had to have water poured down its reluctant throat before it could make up its mind to send a stream of icy spring water gushing out over its protruding lip. The Sandwich glass spoon holder and sugar bowl sat on the red-checked tablecloth that covered the long table. I can still smell the aroma rising in a cloud of steam from the ironstone soup tureen which often graced Grandmother's table. The stove was a big, black range with a copper reservoir at one end for heating water. The oven of the old range seemed always to be sending forth tantalizing aromas—

Indian pudding, the great pot of Saturday-night beans, apple dumplings—and the pies!

Grandmother's pies were not the dainty chiffon concoctions nor lattice-covered delicacies we make today. Her pies were—well, *sturdy* seems a good word to describe them.

Apple pie headed the list: deep apple pie with a tender, flaky crust filled with apple slices smothered in syrup akin to ambrosia. And Grandmother's mincemeat pie was something to remember. Venison was its base, with plenty of apples. Into the simmering mincemeat kettle went a little of everything on the pantry shelves: boiled cider, butter, currant jelly, plump raisins, strong coffee, and spices which she alone knew how to measure.

Then there were the squash and pumpkin pies, open-faced, golden beauties that tasted even better than they looked. Enriched with eggs and cream, they were a rare dessert.

When blueberries were in season, Grandmother baked them in pies which oozed syrup through the holes in their crusts. Red raspberries also made a pie special with their unforgettable flavor. And Grandmother's strawberry pies could be smelled in the back pasture, where my brothers and sisters and I were prying off spruce gum. That wonderful aroma made us hurry home. These pies tasted of sun and wind and rain, with a dash of dew for good measure.

When the hens laid well, we had custard pies. These had a delicate sprinkling of nutmeg on top. The spice was grated on a little tin grater that had a small compartment on top for storing the round, hard nutmeg. Grandmother's custard pie melted in the mouth and left an insatiable desire for more.

As spring gently caressed the earth, the rhubarb poked up from the ground. I can still see Grandmother cutting up the long, green and ruby stalks and still smell their pungent fragrance. Rhubarb pie had the taste of spring itself.

"Pie timber" is what Grandmother called all the ingredients that went into her pies. In the long, narrow buttery she would get out her big cooking board, the pail of lard, the crock of salt, and dip into the flour barrel with her ironstone cup. The lard was worked into the flour by hand and moistened with icy spring water. The floury rolling pin smoothed out rounds of dough. When the pie was filled and covered, Grandmother would skillfully cut away the surplus dough on the edge by holding the pie up in one hand and running a "case knife" around it. The little strip of dough would spiral downward around her arm.

A lovely place, that old buttery: the long shelves held tinware, spatterware, saleratus and sugar firkins, little boxes of spice, cinnamon sticks, sage, and bay leaves. There were blue-flowered Bennington crocks of flat doughnuts and molasses cookies and, beneath the shelves, brown jugs of vinegar and molasses. Even the buttery floor was intriguing, made of wide white pine boards, smoothed and hollowed from constant travel, with lovely brown knots rising here and there. The boards squeaked and so did Grandmother's shoes as she went to and fro singing the old songs she knew.

Photograph by Jessie Walker.

"Hail, Columbia, Happy Land," she sang as she rolled her pie crust. "Rock of Ages" accompanied the stirring of a creamy pie filling. "Sweet Rosalie, the Prairie Flower" still lingers in the flavor of pumpkin pie, and I am sure "Kind Words Can Never Die" echoed in the fragrant steam from simmering fruits.

After a hearty breakfast of pancakes and sausage, or fried salt pork and browned potatoes, with buttermilk biscuits on the side, Grandfather always had room for a wedge of pie. He claimed that the point of each piece just naturally fitted in among the other "vittles."

The recipes for most of Grandmother's pies were unwritten, for she measured a pinch of this, a smidgen of that, a dab of butter, or a blob of molasses. Her pies were treasures our family shared. It seemed to me, as a child, that my grandmother's pies would make a necklace long enough to circle the earth.

A Mother's Picture

Edmund Clarence Stedman

She seemed an angel to our infant eyes!
Once, when the glorifying moon revealed
Her who at evening by our pillow kneeled—
Soft-voiced and golden-haired, from holy skies
Flown to her loves on wings of Paradise—
We looked to see the pinions half-concealed.
The Tuscan vines and olives will not yield
Her back to me, who loved her in this wise,
And since have little known her, but have grown
To see another mother, tenderly,
Watch over sleeping darlings of her own.
Perchance the years have changed her; yet alone
This picture lingers: still she seems to me
The fair, young Angel of my infancy.

The Portrait in My Heart

Ida Driskell Baird

The portrait that I hold most dear of all,
I hide away where others cannot see.
I cherish it down deep within my heart,
Engraved upon my page of memory.
The portrait is my mother, years ago:
The patient, gentle face, the low-bent head,
Humming a tune, the while her fingers flew
That we, her children, might be clothed and fed.
All other memories around her revolve;
The countless mass of lesser things—
The smooth white drifts of winter's snows,
The summer sun, the green of springs,
The birds, the flowers, the dusty lanes,
The autumn woods we loved to roam—
Are but the setting, but the frame
For her. She made our house a home.

A lady's dressing table features a tray with a collection of silver dressing jars and perfume bottles. Photograph by Jessie Walker.

Devotions from the Heart

Pamela Kennedy

Forgetting what is behind and straining toward what is ahead, I press on toward the goal to win the prize for which God has called me heavenward in Christ Jesus.
—Philippians 3:13b–14 (NIV)

LOOKING FORWARD

It has been over a decade since our first child left the nest, and our third one flew the coop about five years ago. I think I have made the transition rather gracefully. But recently we have had the task of cleaning out my parents-in-law's home, and the job fell to me to take down all the photos lining the stairway.

This was no small task. The stairway walls from the basement to the first floor were covered with framed photographs of the family. There were over one hundred snapshots and studio portraits covering five generations. You can't sort through pictures like that very quickly. Although I have walked up and down those stairs innumerable times in the past forty years, there were things I had never noticed.

A yellowed photo of my mother-in-law with her mother and grandmother revealed how alike were their eyes and cheeks and chins. My husband and his younger brother are both retired navy captains, and pictures of them in their military uniforms had a special place on the stairwell wall. But my favorite shot of the two brothers was the one taken of them about fifty years ago as they sat together on the floor playing with their trucks. They were decked out in striped T-shirts and corduroy pants secured with suspenders, caught in a moment of childhood concentration.

There were wedding and baby photos, as well as pictures chronicling the years of each grandchild's life from birth to college graduation. It was these that brought my thoughts back to my own children and made me question just how

Dear Lord, let me not dwell in the memories of my past, but help me to face the future with expectation and courage, eager to find the blessings You have planned for me there. Amen.

well I was doing with the transition from family home to empty nest.

It is so easy to look back, prompted by a photograph, and recollect the events of the past. The teenager standing with bravado on his customized skateboard masked the insecurity of youth. The Little Leaguer in his bright blue uniform brought memories of skinned knees and bruised egos. Photographs of dance recitals, plays,

A single evening primrose is surrounded by sand verbena in Borrego Valley, California. Photograph by Carr Clifton.

and prom nights reminded me of our daughter's frantic rush to be picture-perfect, beautifully turned out, and look confident in the bargain.

There are so many memories, and with them, a hint of regret as well. Did I listen enough and laugh enough? Were there times when my words were too harsh or too critical? Could I have been more understanding? Should I have given in or held out longer when the boundaries were pushed?

I looked at the more recent photographs of my three children as adults, and there was a small sadness in my heart. The time to influence them, to train and teach them, is past. I think I am wiser now. I have been bruised a bit by life myself, and I think I have more compassion than I used to have. But with children you don't get a do-over.

That's why the above verse from Paul's letter to the Philippians comforts me. He had some regrets about his life too. He wondered if maybe he could have done things differently. But then he recognized that what is done, is done, and the only opportunity for growth lies in the future. Life continues, and we can use the days we have to look back, wishing we could change things, or we can move on and improve things.

Paul reminds us that there are still great goals to be achieved and victories to be won. Moving on with hope and courage demands faith that God's promises are true and that what he has planned for us is beyond our greatest expectations. The pictures of the past hold wonderful memories, but sometimes we need to be reminded that in the future there are opportunities to create beautiful portraits as well.

Mater Amabilis

Emma Lazarus

Crowned or crucified—the same
 Glows the flame
Of her deathless love divine.
Still the blessed mother stands,
 In all lands,
As she watched beside thy cradle and by mine.

Whatso gifts the years bestow,
 Still men know,
While she breathes, lives one who sees
(Stand they pure or sin-defiled)
 But the child
Whom she crooned to sleep and rocked upon her knees.

And as in childhood, so throughout our lives—
the mother is the very core, cornerstone, and
foundation upon which the true Christian home is
built and the center about which it revolves.
Through all the years of our lives, we will carry
with us those lessons of patience and fortitude; of
long-suffering and forgiveness; of love and affection that the typical Christian mother by her
word and act, by her precept and example, teaches
her children. Just consider for a moment the dignity and tenderness and grandeur of this wonderful thing called mother-love. This is why the
philosophers have said that the future of society
and of the human race itself rests in large measure
on the strength and character, virtue and nobility
of the mothers of the world.

—Joseph T. Karcher

*The floating blooms of white irises and the velvety touch of lamb's ear are only two fea-
tures of a walk through this garden. Photograph by Larry LeFever/Grant Heilman.*

To a Mother

Marion Doyle

There is a road that leads to you,
No matter where you are,
A little path to love and home
Beneath the evening star—
That wistful little winding way
That's beautiful and wise,
That leads me to your waiting heart,
Your smile, your shining eyes.

Remembered Years

May Smith White

Who does not long to go back home again
Where greening hills flow down to meet a stream
And rippling music stirs to life a dream
Half-hidden in the moment's tangled skein?
Forgetting all of fickle youth's disdain,
To lie submerged in magic from the gleam
Of some remembered moon and trace the scheme
Of rapture is a power that will sustain.

May I forever hold the ripened years
Against my breast, an ever-shining shield,
Recalling how each treasured hour unlocks
A door that leads beyond the moment's fears.
Who does not long and dare, at least to yield
To his desire for home and hollyhocks!

Tidytips and California goldfields decorate this area of the Carrizo Plain National Monument, in the San Joaquin Valley of California. Photograph by Terry Donnelly/Donnelly Austin Photography.

Remember Mother

Esther York Burkholder

All our lives, let us remember Mother.
When we are sad or hurt,
    may we remember her loving arms and be comforted.
When we are happy,
    let us share joy with her in recollection.
When we are ill,
    may we remember her tender care for our childhood ills and
    be srengthened.
When we are tempted to do wrong,
    let us recall her wise guidance and her prayers in our behalf.
When we fail,
    may her memory give us courage to try again.
When we succeed,
    may we see again the pride in her eyes.

Remember Mother with devotion while she lives and with loving
memory when she is gone. But always—remember Mother!

*My mother was an angel on earth. She was a minister of
blessing to all human beings within her sphere of action.
Her heart was the abode of heavenly purity. She had no
feelings but of kindness and beneficence, yet her mind
was as firm as her temper was mild and gentle.*
—John Quincy Adams

*A flowering crab apple tree is a focal point in this garden
in Owen Sound, Canada. Photograph by Darryl R. Beers.*

To My Mother

Eugene Field

How fair you are, my mother!
    Ah, though 'tis many a year
    Since you were here,
Still do I see your beauteous face,
    And with the glow
Of your dark eyes cometh a grace
    Of long ago.
So gentle, too, my mother!
    Just as of old, upon my brow,
    Like benedictions now,
Falleth your dear hand's touch;
    And still, as then,
A voice that glads me overmuch
    Cometh again,
My fair and gentle mother!
How you have loved me, Mother,
    I have not power to tell,
    Knowing full well
That even in the rest above
    It is your will
To watch and guard me with your love,
    Loving me still.
And, as of old, my mother,
    I am content to be a child,
    By mother's love beguiled
From all these other charms;
    So to the last
Within thy dear, protecting arms
    Hold thou me fast,
My guardian angel, Mother!

A mother and daughter enjoy an outing in this painting entitled ROSES AND LILIES by American artist Mary L. Fairchild MacMonnies (1858–1956). Image from Art Resource, NY/Musée des Beaux-Arts, Rouen, France. Photograph by Erich Lessing.

READERS' FORUM

Snapshots from our IDEALS readers

Left: "Who needs rain?" Three-and-a-half-year-old Madisen and her sister, Lauren, six, posed for this picture with their grandmother's umbrella. They are the daughters of Kal and Shelby Larson of Bismarck, North Dakota, and the grandchildren of Duane and Shirley Larson of Bottineau, North Dakota.

Below Left: "So pretty!" Two-year-old Kayla McKenzie Whitis enjoys the flowers in Grandmother Janine Whitis's garden in Louisville, Kentucky. Kayla is the daughter of Kyle and Brenda Whitis. Her grandparents, Orvil and Barbara Flick of Freeland, Indiana, and Great-Grandmother Catherine Jane Whitis of Corydon, Indiana, all dote on her every chance they have.

Below: "No more birthday gifts as long as I live," happily declared Great-Grandmother Myrtle Lepler of Clara City, Minnesota, when she and Great-Grandfather August received the news of Kaitlyn Elizabeth Lepler's arrival on Myrtle's birthday.

Left: Miniature "Muscle Man," Trevor William O'Malley, is the grandson of Ralph and Louise Johnson of Bartlett, Tennessee. His parents are J.J. and Tammy O'Malley of North Carolina.

Below Left: Two-year-old Brett loves his ToTo, given to him by his aunt, Betty Maze. He is the son of Garry and Alice Word and grandson of Marcelene Debard, all of Mountain City, Tennessee.

Below: Cousins David and Nicole were born five days apart and have already become buddies. They are the grandchildren of David and Cathy Andrews of Milford, New Hampshire.

Dear Reader,

My mother was the youngest child in her family and had to learn to defend herself well against siblings at an early age. Not only was she adept at verbal combat, but also she would stand firm, literally, until she was clearly understood. Many times she maintained that stiff, upright position in front of me to emphasize the inappropriateness of my behavior. But instead of growing up intimidated, I learned, in my turn, to admire strength of conviction in women. My high school and college years were tumultuous; there were many changes occurring in society. But I always had the memory of my mother, with shoulders held back and chin tilted up, to encourage me to believe in my own ideas and make my own decisions.

My mother also taught me that life is so much more pleasant when people are gracious to others, that cooking is another art form, and that the commonplace lives of woodpeckers, squirrels, and other critters inhabiting our backyards are fascinating opportunities for laughter and learning. She even had compassion for grackles—which nobody else I ever knew liked—because they flew with red-winged blackbirds.

Mother grew up in Oklahoma and brought to her new home in Tennessee a practical approach to solving everyday problems, but also a love of fine art and Puccini and long novels that are worth staying up late to finish.

Today I see her blue-eyed determination in my son's face after hours of strenuous basketball practice, and I see her strong chin line in my daughter's decision to move West in her early twenties.

Thank you, Mother, for all those demands you made for As in school and for providing an example of dignity that inspires me today.

An armful of roses to all mothers and the memories of mothers on this special day,

Marjorie L. Lloyd

ideals

Publisher, Patricia A. Pingry
Editor, Marjorie Lloyd
Designer, Royce DeGrie
Copy Editors, Melinda Rathjen, Nancy Skarmeas
Permissions Editor, Patsy Jay
Contributing Writers, Lansing Christman, Joan Donaldson, Pamela Kennedy, D. Fran Morley, Arlene Siebold, Connie Wetzell

ACKNOWLEDGMENTS

CHRISTMAN, LANSING. "Friend To a Song Sparrow." from *Harp Strings In the Wind.* Copyright © 1998 by Lansing Christman and Nancy Ogle. Used by permission. CROWELL, GRACE NOLL. "Ageless Motherhood" from *Let the Sun Shine In.* Copyright © 1970. Published by Fleming Revell Co. Used by permission of the Baker Publishing Group. JAQUES, EDNA "These Things Are Good" from *Aunt Hattie's Place* by Edna Jaques, published by Thomas Allen, Ltd. Copyright © 1949. Used by permission of Louise Bonnell. JOHNSON, MARGARET. "Day Dreams" from *Best Loved Poems of the American People.* TATUM, EDITH. "Treasures" from *The Virginian-Pilot,* 1927. Used here without objection. Our sincere thanks to those authors, or their heirs, who submitted poems or essays to IDEALS for publication. Every possible effort has been made to acknowledge ownership of material used.

Inside back cover: The sun tips the petals of these lovely flowers with light in this painting entitled SHADOWS AND REFLECTIONS by Boris Nicolaiev. Image from Fine Art Photographic Library, Ltd., London/Walker Gallery Harrogate/Gallery Gerard, Wassenaar, Holland.